MORE THAN A
Conqueror
Triumph over Tragedy

EVANGELIST ARMETHA INGRAM

authorHOUSE®

AuthorHouse™
1663 Liberty Drive
Bloomington, IN 47403
www.authorhouse.com
Phone: 1 (800) 839-8640

Published by AuthorHouse 02/05/2018

ISBN: 978-1-5462-2668-0 (sc)
ISBN: 978-1-5462-2667-3 (e)

Contents

Dedication

I, Evangelist Armetha Ingram, dedicate my book of poetry, entiled, "MORE THAN A CONQUEROR," to my son, Benjamin S.M. Ingram, my family, my mother, Louise Ingram. My sisters, Annie and Nancy and my brothers, Charlie and Michael, my Pastors, Bishop L.C. Young, Aposyle Cleveland Smith, my Prophet, Prophet Peter Popoff, all of my Brethren, and my good friend, Helen Ellison, as well as other friends, and relatives.

About The Author

About me

I am a Christian Freelance Writer who have been writing since I was ten, and I have written a Wealth of poetry, plays, Including a Screen Play, Short Stories, Songs, A Human Interest Story, Commercials, and whatever. The Lord leads me to write. I have poetry published in various Anthologies Of Poetry, and also on an Album, as well as two CD's, entitled, THE SOUNDS OF POETRY, and read to Beautiful, Classic, Baroque Music, by a professional. The Album, and CD, is Compliments of ILLIAD PRESS. However, I have poetry published in Anthologies OF POETRY, by ILLIAD PRESS, and WORLD OF POETRY PRESS. I have written over two hundred songs to date, and I am presently done two Demo CD'S, a Single, and a regular CD. My Short Stories consist of a variety, in which my Short Story, entitled, NO, won Second Place in a Literary Arts Contest. In addition, I have written a wealth of Plays, in which most have been Performed at my Church, in which one was directed by my Former Pastor. One Play was performed as a Dinner Theatre, with proceeds of thirty-five dollars a ticket going to a Charity Benefit. This Play was entitled, A DAY IN THE LIFE OF A VIRTEOUS WOMAN. Presently I have written a Screen Play which is entitled, THE RAPTURE OF THE CHURCH-THIS WORLD IS NOT MY HOME, to be used as a Movie. I also need to make mention of the fact that I have written numerous Commercials in which my Chiropractor, friend used one for his BUSINESS, causing his BUSINESS to prosper to the point of having to get a Partner. I also have written a HUMAN INTEREST STORY for THE MOBILE PRESS REGISTER. I ALSO HAVE A CD ENTITLED, "MORE THAN A MIRACLE, "EVANGELIST ARMETHA INGRAM, AND THE WEBSITE IS: http://www.cdbaby/cd/evangelistarmethaingram.

Song Of My Heart

BY: *Evangelist Armetha Ingram*

I will lift up my voice, and sing.
I'm more than a conqueror; I'm a child of THE KING.

Through every battle that has been fought,
It was not on my own, that victory was wrought.

But my GOD, ALMIGHTY GOD, has always fought for me.
HE has given me the victory, on every hand, you see.

This song of my heart, tells the story.
I'm more than a conqueror; I give my GOD, THE GLORY.

God Has It All In Control

BY Evangelist Armetha Ingram

GOD HAS IT ALL IN CONTROL," CAME TO MIND.
I Thank YOU O' LORD For Causing Everything To Work Out Fine.

I know that nothing is too hard for GOD, or too big for HIM.
HE controls all situations, and light my path when it seems dim.

GOD is Omnipotent, And Omnipresent,
All Knowing, And Everywhere.
So no matter where your problem lies, GOD is right there.

So don't take matters in your own hand, for only GOD knows best.
Do You Not Know That GOD Is In Control Of Every Trial, And Test?

HE tells us to Cast Our Cares Upon HIM, For HE Cares For Us.
So why let dire situations cause you to make a fuss?

GOD has the whole World, and Universe in HIS HANDS.
HE Just wants Us To Live By HIS Commands.

GOD Has Always Proven HIMSELF To Me.
HE Brings Me Forth As Pure Gold Tried In The Fire, Don't You See?

GOD wants to prove HIMSELF to the entire nation, and World.
Yes, GOD wants to prove HIMSELF to
every man, woman, boy, and girl.

We are living "IN THE LATTER DAYS", whereas there is much unrest.
We are living in a time whereas we must possess what we confess.

For satan's army is on the rampage.
For a planetary takeover, they are setting the stage.
Let Us Take A Stand, not bowing to satan's rage.

With their NEW WORLD ORDER AGENDA to destroy
Christianity, our GOD GIVEN, and HUMAN RIGHTS.
With this in mind, we must fight "THE GOOD FIGHT."

We must Keep The Faith, and appeal to our
HUMAN RIGHTS ORGANIZATION.
Overall, Know That GOD Is In Control, therefore let us have patience.

After we have done all to stand, stand anyhow.
To satan's NEW WORLD ORDER, don't even dare bow.

For GOD Has It All In Control.
So let Us Trust HIM, Just As The Patriots Of Old.

Ending New World Order Corruption

BY: Evangelist Armetha Ingram

THE NEW WORLD ORDER destroys Humanity, and Christianity.
It creates a world of total chaos, and insanity.

It eliminates all GOD GIVEN RIGHTS,
FREEDOM, AND HUMAN RIGHTS.
To Genocide, and destroy Humanity, are the AntiChrist's plights.

The Reptillian Race are wrecking havoc in the world.
Their goal is to eliminate every man, woman, boy, and girl.

God is in control; Satan, and his army is defeated. God
will, and is, raising up His people unseated.

God's Mighty Warriors are fighting the Good Fight Of Faith.
We are walking in The Will Of God, being obedient to what He saith.

God wants His people to cry loud, and spare not,
To expose injustice, and NWO corruption, giving it all we've got.

We The People must appeal to our HUMAN
RIGHTS ORGANIZATIONS,
Meanwhile we must also appeal to our Legislation.

The Government collaborates with NEW
WORLD ORDER as Researched.
They keep it clandestine, dumbing down the public, and Church.

The well being of our Planet Earth is at stake.
We must be about our Father's Bussiness, for Christ's sake.

Humanity, as a whole, need to get involved.
God uses People, Not Rocks, to get the problem solved.

Seeing Eye To Eye

BY: Evangelist Armetha Ingram

Is it a debate?
Or is it animosity, and hate?

One can agree, or dissagree.
To opinionate is free.

Is it fault finding?
Or is it bussiness minding?

Everyone ought to look at one's self.
Then one would'nt point the finger at everyone else.

One tell the other not to say a word.
Then one spread gossip about what one heard.

Someone just might be gossipping about you too.
Treat others the way that you want them to treat you.

Don't hold a grudge for not seeing eye to eye.
Garbage belongs in the can, so bid garbage bringers good-by.

Make sure your life is lined up with THE WORD OF GOD ABOVE
Make sure that you are walking in HIS AGAPE LOVE.

Let GOD reveal HIMSELF to you.
Then HE will let you know what to do.

All you have to do is wait on GOD, with patience.
HE will direct you in handling all situations.

I Count It All Joy

BY: Evangelist Armetha Ingram

I count it all joy when I am suffering for Christ's sake.
I count it all joy when I go through divers trials to make.

I realize that great is my reward in Heaven.
Yet on this earth, God is with me twenty-four seven.

I count it all joy when my body is racking with pain.
I count it all joy when my living for God is counted vain.

I have Abundant life through the Cross that Jesus bare.
So in every situation, I can count on Him to be right there.

Sometimes I have to go through the storm and rain.
Yet there are great benefits that the sufferings contain.

So I always rest in God, and count it all joy.
I welcome these benefits, not letting these sufferings anoy.

8

Bought And Sold Out

BY Evangelist Armetha Ingram

I've been bought with a price that only Jesus could pay,
His own Blood as sacrifice, to wash my sins away.

He bleed upon the Cross you see,
He did it for you and I.

Gave His life to set us free,
That we would'nt have to die.

Of all that I am, or that I ever hope to be,
I owe it all to The Precious Lamb, who gave His life for me.

I owe You Lord my all in all, and more to You is due.
I'll ever listen for Your call, I'm sold out to You.

Let God Exalt You

BY: Evangelist Armetha Ingram

So many are tripping over the other to get ahead.
They'll scheme, and trample over you 'till you're dead.

Everybody is trying so hard to outdo one another.
You find it in every race, not just a sister, or brother.

What's with all of this trying to keep up with the Jones?
If the Jones jumped off a bridge, and you did too, you'll be gone.

So all of the rat racing to get ahead is absolute vanity.
The things people do to get ahead is total insanity.

A Word to the so called wise:
Rest in God, and let Him control your life.

If you are humble, The Lord will exalt you in due time.
Be faithful and patient, and everything will work out fine.

Life

BY: *Evangelist Armetha Ingram*

Life does not consist of the things we posess.
However, Life is defined in True Holiness.

In God, we live, we move, and have our being.
So one might say that this is life, or so it seem.

For God's breath caused man to become a living soul.
However Life is a sheep that has come into the Fold.

Outside of Our Great Shepherd's Fold, one is merely existing.
We are defined as one of God's creations in this listing.

To become a Child Of God, herein is life.
So I Thank Almighty God that His Amazing Grace suffice.

One may possess material goods, and friends, without end.
Yet life only exist when one is washed of his sin.

For these temporal things will pass away.
But God's Word is Eternal; It is here to stay.

So to be a Child Of God, herein is Life manifested.
Being God's Child, our Agape Love will be proven and tested.

This is so that our Life will stay lined up with The Word.
For I for one was merely existing, and it is so absurd.

Salvation Summed Up

BY: Evangelist Armetha Ingram

Salvation can be summed up in adding righteousness.
It can be summed up by subtracting unrighteousness.

Multiplying is growing in Grace and Knowledge OF JESUS CHRIST.

We divide ourselves, being in the world, but not of the world.

Welcome The Rain

BY:Evangelist Armetha Ingram

Some things may not go the way that you think that they should.
Welcome the rain, for all things work for your good.

GOD does all things well, and with a purpose in mind.
Just have patience, and everything will work out fine.

Like a puzzle, pieces of your chaotic life will come together.
Then you will see GOD'S MASTER PLAN better.

So welcome the rain, for there is so much to gain.
Know that GOD is taking you to a higher plane.

After the rain, the sun will come shining through.
On the other side of the rain, is a rainbow of blessings for you.

Let Patience Have Her Perfect Work In Your Life

BY: Evangelist Armetha Ingram

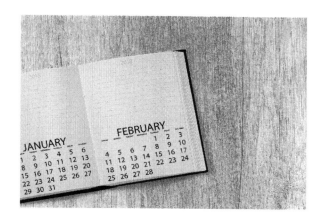

Let Patience Have Her Perfect Work In Your Life,
For on The Cross Of Calvary, Jesus has already paid the Price.

Be it known unto you, that whatever God
has promised, He will surely bring to pass.
So be faithful in The Will of God, and above all, be ye steadfast.

Don't get weary along the way.
A thousand years to God, is but a day.

So continue ye in The Lord; Don't quit.
My God will move when He sees fit.

So don't take matters in your own hand, but wait.
My GOD is never, ever late.

Note:

Bought, And Sold Out," and "Let Patience Have Her Perfect Work In Your Life,"
were also published in Anthologies Of Poetry, and recorded on an Album, and CD to Beautiful, Classic Baroque Music, and read by a Professional, with other poets' poems included on this Album, and CD, as well.

From The Beginning, I Have Won!

Evangelist Armetha Ingram

Saved, and sanctified, Holy Ghost-Filled, and Baptised.
I've got my war clothes on; In God's Love, I abide.

Devil, you do'nt want to mes with me; You know I'm not the one.
You are defeated from the beginning; From the beginning, I have won!

So Why Not Give Your Life To The Lord?

BY: Evangelist Armetha Ingram

Christ died for you, and I, on Calvary.
He gave His Precious Life to set us free.
So why not give your life to The Lord?
This world has nothing to offer you.
Christ offers you Life, brand new.
So why not give your life to The Lord?
Let Christ take up residence inside.
Let His Love within you abide.
So why not give your life to The Lord?
The Coming Of Christ draweth nigh.
Bid worldly pleasures,"Good-by."
So why not give your life to The Lord?

Stand Strong O' Weather Beaten Rock

BY: Evangelist Armetha Ingram

Stand strong, and tall, o' weather beaten rock, stand tall.
The weather will not change you, come Winter Spring Summer, or Fall.

You have stood down through the years.
You knew no pain; You knew no fears.

God enables me to stand, and I shall not be moved, no never.
He equips me to stand; He has been with me forever.

Although I count it all joy, through the sufferings, there have been some tears.
Yet God kept me standing through it all, down through the years.

The Raging River

BY: Evangelist Armetha Ingram

Sometimes life is like A Raging River.
Oh, but I know a Strong Deliverer.

So, irregardless as to how chaotic your life might be,
I know The One who calms the River, Ocean, and Sea.

Just trust in Him, to see you through,
For He knows just what to do.
The One who I am speaking of,
Is none other than MY GOD above.

The Winds Wraps Her Arms Around The Golden Wheat

BY: Evangelist Armetha Ingram

The *winds wraps her arms around the golden wheat.*
It never worries about tomorrow, or what it will eat.

God clothe the animals, and sends rain to the grain.
He's my Provider, for He never change.

So whatever I need, I cast my cares upon Him.
And He wraps His loving arms around me even when my way seems dim.

My Guardian Angel

BY: Evangelist Armetha Ingram

For He shall give His Angels charge over you to keep you in all your ways.
They shall bear you up in their hands, lest you dash your
foot against a stone, is what The Scriptures says.

God's Angels are sent by God to guard me each day.
These Angels keep watch, and protect me from harm's way.
I Truly thank My God, for His Divine Protection,
And I'll forever thank My God for how He leads,
and guides me, in the Right Direction.

What Is A Friend?

BY: Evangelist Armetha Ingram

Jesus, The Greatest Friend ever to possess,
Is also the One who loves me best.

He sticks closer to me than a brother,
And has been to me, more than a mother.

When all of my so call friends were gone,
Jesus never forsook me, or left me alone.

Through tribulation, and despair,
I could count on Him to be right there.

When scorned, and abused,
Lied on, and misused,

I never, ever doubted,
That My Jesus knew all about it.

And I shall never fail to confess,
That Jesus has proven Himself to me, through every trial, and test.

Yes, He's been there through thick, and thin,
Oh, how I thank my God for my Best Friend!

The Ocean

BY: *Evangelist Armetha Ingram*

*The Ocean is peace, and tranquility, and oh so wide.
In God, I found a special peace, for in Him, I abide.*

*I found Agape Love, in Him, that's wider than the ocean.
I love Him with my whole heart, soul, and
mind, for I give Him my devotion.*

*For God's Love for me is wider than any ocean, or sea,
God has given me favor, and in His Will is the safest place to be.*

The Winds, And The Waves

Evangelist Armetha Ingram

The winds, and the waves might beat vehemetedly, sometimes, in my life,
Yet I can rest assured, that God's Grace will suffice.
He speaks to the winds, and rain; They have to stand still.
For Heaven, Earth, and The Universe, have to obey God's Will.
For God has it all in control.
So all I have to do, is rest in Him; Let the story be told.

Beyond The Walls

BY: Evangelist Armetha Ingram

Beyond the walls of GOD'S SANCTUARY,
SALVATION must yet abide.
For it does not end in THE HOUSE OF
GOD, but we take it on the outside.

After the singing has ceased, the band has stopped
playing, and every prayer has been prayed,
Beyond the walls, awaits our opportunity, for the
FRUIT OF THE SPIRIT to be portrayed.

People are dying everywhere, for they hunger for THE WORD.
We can bring LIFE to these hungry souls,
by living what we have heard.

We live it at home, on the job, on the streets, and everywhere we go.
If the world doesn't see CHRIST in us, how else will they know?

People namely can be won, by watching how we treat one another.
Then they know that we are GOD'S DESCIPLES,
because we love our brother.

The Champion

BY: Evangelist Armetha Ingram

Once a champion, always a champion,
because I am living for THE LORD.
For a CHILD OF GOD is never defeated, abiding in HIS WORD.

When my back is against the wall,
Or when I am alone, in left field, and the enemy
is watching, and waiting for me to fall,

That is the right time, for me to hold on, and run on, even the more.
For I'm the champion; I never loose, but always score.

What then, can I say, but draw this conclusion.
I'm the champion; Defeat in my life, is only an illusion.

If you think that I boast, you're right, because I do.
For I Boast (GLORY) in MY LORD, AND SAVIOR, JESUS
CHRIST, and if you're a champion, you will too!

I Won't Turn Back

BY: Evangelist Armetha Ingram

(Like a tree planted by the rivers of waters, I shall not be moved)

Though storms beat against my soul,
And though the enemy comes up against me, so bold,
I won't turn back.

Though the waves of persecution, against me, roar,
And though my body may be racking with pain, and oh so sore,
I won't turn back.

Though trials come on every hand,
And though my affliction might seem as grains of sand,
I won't turn back.

For I realize that GOD has it all in control,
And HE will deliver me, as the patriots of old.

For HE has proven HIMSELF over, and over again,
And HE has always helped me to stand.

So, no matter what I endure, this is TRUTH, and fact,
I'm a living witness, I won't turn back!

Wake Up In The Morning, With A Smile On Your Face

Evangelist Armetha Ingram

Wake up in the morning with a smole on ypur face.
You ought to be concerned about what my GOD says.

When GOD causes you to arise,
As soon as you open your eyes,

You ought to THANK THE LORD that a
brand new day has just begun.
You ought to THANK HIM for giving you
HIS ONLY BEGOTTEN SON.

Let HIS PRAISES be uttered from your lips.
THANK THE LORD for in HIM, your beautiful relationship.

As you continue to communicate, and relate,
I serve you notice, that MY GOD, is never late.

As you continue to go about your day,
Obey all that MY GOD say.

Then you will experience manifest victory,
that has already been designed
!in your Destiny.

Give Us O' Lord, Our Daily Bread

BY: *Evangelist Armetha Ingram*

(PREEMINENCE)

Give us O' LORD, our DAILY BREAD.
O' LORD, YOU will perform, just what YOU said.

For OUR DAILY BREAD, is not just physical, but SPIRITUAL.
No, it's not just a consumption of a physical food ritual.

But it is THE FRUIT OF THE SPIRIT, which is LOVE,
PEACE, and JOY, IN THE HOLY GHOST.
THESE GODLY ATTRIBUTES, we need the MOST.

O' LORD YOU have all THINGS PERTAINING
TO LIFE, AND GODLINESS.
And YOU always know for us, what is BEST.

For YOUR EYES are on the sparrow, and
we know YOU WATCHES US.
So, we don't have to be overly concerned about physical stuff.

For as we seek YOUR RIGHTEOUSNESS,
our needs, YOU WILL FULLFILL.
For it has already been designed, in YOUR PREDESTINED WILL.

Lord, I Surrender My Life Unto You

BY: *Evangelist Armetha Ingram*

(Like a tree planted by the rivers of waters, I shall not be moved.)

LORD, I surrender my life unto YOU.
Have THINE OWN WAY, LORD; THINE WILL I'll do.

My life DEAR LORD, is no longer mine,
But my entire life, is wholly THINE.

Use my feet LORD, each and every day.
LORD, let me walk, in THY RIGHTEOUS WAY.

Use my hands LORD, just to do THINE WILL,
While I am waiting, LORD, yielded, and still.

My life DEAR LORD, YOU now hold.
So, HAVE YOUR WAY; It's YOURS to mold.

(Like a tree, planted by the rivers of waters, I shall not be moved.)

Why Are You Afraid?

Evangelist Armetha Ingram

Why are you afraid?
Is it because of your lack of LOVE, that has caused
you to get angry at someone, in some way,
To make their lives miserable, and to ruin their day?

You slandered Sue, and lied on Jack.
You talked about Ola, behind her back.

You told Trudy to listen, and not to say a word,
While you told her something about Lydia, you just heard.

But the same people whom you persecuted, and hurt,
Treated you kind, instead of like dirt.

And now you are no longer full of mirth, and fun.
But you are running, as though someone is chasing you with a gun.

You wonder, "Why are they so kind?
They act as if everything is fine.

If you have THE LOVE OF GOD, in your life,
And if you are not filled with strife,

Then, you will not have to run,
Because of all the bad things you have done.

You will not live a life that is defeated.
But you will treat others, the way you wish to be treated!

(What Would JESUS Do?)

I'm Gonna Hold On To My Testimony

BY Evangelist Armetha Ingram (WRITTEN: APRIL 2009) NOTE:(((COULD BE ON SUNDAY'S BEST)

(Like a tree, planted by the rivers of waters, I shall not be moved.)

1. I'M GOMMA HOLD ON TO MY
TESTIMONY, AND I WON'T LET GO.
I WON'T LOOK TO THE RIGHT, NOR LEFT,
O' LORD, BECAUSE I LOVE YOU SO!

YES, I'VE GOT MY HAND IN GOD'S HAND, AND
I'M GONNA LIVE BY HIS COMMAND.
AND I THANK YOU O' LORD, FOR HELPING ME TO STAND.

FOR I'M ON MY WAY TO GLORY; YES,
I'VE GOT HEAVEN IN MY VIEW.
AND I THANK YOU, O' LORD, FOR MAKING
ME ONE OF YOUR CHOSEN FEW!

2. I'M GONNA HOLD ON TO MY
TESTIMONY, AND I WON'T LET GO!
YOU'VE DONE SO MUCH FOR ME O' LORD,
EVEN BEFORE YOU SAVED MY SOUL!

AND, EVERY SINCE THAT DAY, YOU JUST KEEP
RIGHT ON OPENING MANY DOORS.
AND I'LL PRAISE YOU, AND LIVE FOR
YOU, O' LORD, FOREVERMORE!

OH, STEADFAST, UNMOVABLE, O' LORD,
I STAND UPON YOUR WORD.
AND I'M SO GLAD, YOUR VOICE, O'
LORD, ONE DAY I HEARD!

3. YES! I'M GONNA HOLD ON TO MY
TESTIMONY, AND I WON'T LET GO!
NO MATTER WHAT THEY SAY,
WHEATHER FRIEND, OR FOE!

FOR I'VE GOT A MADE UP MIND, O'
LORD, TO GO ALL THE WAY!
AND NO MATTER WHAT YOUR WILL
IS, O' LORD, I'M GONNA OBEY!

FOR I DELIGHT TO DO THY WILL O' LORD,
NO MATTER WHAT IT MAY BE!
AND NO MATTER WHAT, O' LORD, YOU CAN COUNT ON ME!

CHORUS:

I'M GONNA HOLD ON TO MY TESTIMONY,
AND I WON'T LET GO!
I'M GONNA HOLD ON TO MY TESTIMONY,
AND I WON'T LET GO!

I'M GONNA HOLD ON TO MY TESTIMONY,
O' LORD, AND I WON'T LET GO!
I'M GONNA HOLD ON TO MY TESTIMONY,
O' LORD, AND I WON'T LET GO!

O' LORD, I'M GONNA HOLD ON TO MY
TESTIMONY, AND I WON'T LET GO!
O' LORD, I'M GONNA HOLD ON TO MY
TESTIMONY, AND I WON'T LET GO!

YES, LORD, I'M GONNA HOLD ON TO MY
TESTIMONY, AND I WON'T LET GO!
YES, LORD, I'M GONNA HOLD ON TO MY
TESTIMONY, AND I WON'T LET GO!

(Like a tree, planted by the rivers of waters, I shall not be moved.)

My Faith Is Under Fire

BY: Evangelist Armetha Ingram

They arrest you for crime that you have not done.
To let them tell it, they are having fun.

They play around with injustice, as a toy belonging to a child.
The JUDICIAL SYSTEM, and the GOVERNMENT,
is corrupt, but to the public, they are in denial.

Surely the devil came to destroy, steal, and kill.
So they set out to do it; Never mind how you feel,

Because we are living in a society, whereas the GOVERNMENT,
and JUDICIAL SYSTEM, does it's own will.
They forget about what GOD wants, and how HE feels.

When GOD SAYS, "Do," the GOVERNMENT says, "Don't."
RIGHTEOUSNESS, and JUSTICE, they don't want.

They are full of criminal activity beyond measure.
It does not mean a thing, for them to kill you for pleasure.

But GOD sits high, and HE looks low.
And there is nothing that HE does not know.

For there is nothing covered, that shall not be uncovered,
and nothing hidden, that shall not be revealed.
So when the corrupt GOVERNMENT and JUDICIAL
SYSTEM fall, it is what GOD has willed.
For GOD'S WORD is settled in HEAVEN; IT is sealed.

For, "Venegenace is MINE," saith THE LORD, "I will repay."
My Faith is under fire, but there's a better day.

My God Is Everything To Me

BY: Evangelist Armetha Ingram

My GOD is everything to me.
There's no other place that I'd rather be,
Than in HIM, WHO freed me from sin.
HE'S THE LIGHTER OF MY PATH, when my way seems dim.

HE'S right there, when I can not see my way.
Then, I am reminded that HE is the way.
I can do nothing without HIM.
HE'LL never leave me out on a limb.

When my back is up against a wall,
I tell you, HE never let me fall.
HE keeps me, and helps me to stand tall.
I tell you, HE'S my ALL IN ALL.

Without HIM, where would I be?
I can do nothing without HIM, you see.
GOD has proven HIMSELF to me,, over, and over again,
Causing me to delight in HIS DIVINE COMMAND.

I love THE LORD, with my whole heart.
I'LL ever be grateful for HIM giving me a brand new start.
I love THE LORD, with my whole soul, and mind.
No matter what I go through, everything works out fine.

For all things work together for the good,
And GOD always delivers me just as HE says HE would.
So I'm a living witness, that no matter what you go through,
My GOD will take good care of you.

Yes, I know without a shadow of a doubt,
. That HE will surely bring you out.
All you have to do, is keep the FAITH,
And just obey what my GOD says.

Just hold on to HIS UNCHANGING HAND
And go on in JESUS NAME.
HE'LL be with you through the rain.
HE'LL be with you through sickness, and pain.

HE will deliver you; HE'S THE STRONG DELIVERER.
MY GOD is more to me than gold, or silver.
I tell you, HE will bring you forth, as pure gold,
Tried in the fire, as the patriots of old.

Yes, MY GOD is EVERYTHING TO ME,
And there's no other place that I'D rather be,
Than in HIM, WHO freed me from sin.
HE'S THE LIGHTER OF MY PATH, when my way seems dim.

Be Ye Steadfast

BY: Evangelist Armetha Ingram

*Be ye steadfast, unmovable, always abounding in THE WORK OF THE LORD, for your
labor in HIM, is not in vain.
As a good soldier, in GOD'S ARMY, we must arm ourselves to endure the suffering, and the pain.
For our SAVIOR suffered likewise, and no servant is greater Than HIS MASTER.
I know that the suffering can not compare to the GLORY to be revealed in the HEREAFTER. (HEAVEN)*

*Know that all things work together for the good, for we are called according to GOD'S PURPOSE IN MIND.
So no matter what we endure, we know that it is going to work out fine.
So let us keep our Hands in GOD'S hand, and hold on in JESUS NAME.
For we serve ALMIGHTY GOD, WHO NEVER CHANGE, BUT
. REMAINS THE SAME*

Victory!

BY: Evangelist Armetha Ingram

As I stood in the window of the building, of my apartment,
I was Thanking YOU O' LORD, for all the many BLESSINGS YOU
Sent.
For you have sent many BLESSINGS my way.
And I THANK YOU O' LORD, for experiencing a better day.

For when I woke up this morning, things did not exactly go my way.
Yet, no matter what, GOD'S WILL, I'm going to obey.
I stood on the stairway, as MY GOD COMMANDED,
And watched the devil steal mail from my box, red- handed.

I rebuked him silently, as I stood right there.
I know the devil was mad, but I didn't care.
I counted each piece of mail, as he put it in my box.
I knew that there was much more than I got.

I knew that he had some hiding in the truck,
And was counting on their (fallen angels) own vain luck,
To bring the rest of my mail, when I was not around.
For the rest of the fallen angels to steal, but I had them bound

So I took the remainder of my mail, that I did receive,
And read a letter, from my Prophet, and did believe,
Everything that GOD had him to say to me.
For it spelled, V-I-C-T-O-R-Y, ABSOLUTE,
PREDESTINED, VICTORY!

Do You Know Him?

BY: Evangelist Armetha Ingram

Do you know HIM, as your SAVIOR?
HE will save your sin sick soul.
HE will cleanse, and make you whole.

Do you know HIM as your HEALER?
HE will heal you of all sickness and disease.
HE will cause all pain in your body to cease.

Do you know HIM, as your DELIVERER?
HE will deliver you from whatever you
are bound with, for HE'S THE
STRONG DELIVERER.

Do you know HIM, as your keeper?
HE will comfort, and keep you, through all situations.
All you have to do, is just have patience.

Do you know HIM, as your FATHER?
HE is the CREATOR of the World, And Entire Universe.
Yet, we become HIS CHILDREN, through SALVATION, and we put
HIM FIRST.

I THANK GOD for THE FATHER, THE
SON, THE HOLY GHOST,
THESE THREE.
For, THEY ARE THE BLESSED TRINITY.
THEY ARE ALL ONE, BUT WITH
DIFFERENT FUNCTIONS, don't you
see?

GOD IS THE CREATOR, AND HE'S ALPHA AND OMEGA, THE
THE BEGINNING AND END.
I THANK HIM for being MY BEST FRIEND,
WHO sticks right there, with me through thick, and thin.

JESUS IS THE SAVIOR, GOD, HIMSELF, INCARNATED IN THE
FLESH, THE ONLY BEGOTTEN SON
OF GOD, WHO laid down HIS
LIFE, for our sins, and WHO now sits at
THE RIGHT HAND OF GOD,
Making intercession for our sins.
JESUS is our ADVOCATE, WHO helps us to make it in.
This is irregardless as to how we have been.

THE HOLY GHOST is our COMFORTER,
and KEEPER, WHO keeps us
Unto THE DAY OF REDEMPTION, and
leads us in all TRUTH, ALL
RIGHTEOUSNESS.
THE HOLY GHOST KEEPS US IN TRUE HOLINESS.
I THANK GOD FOR HIS UNCONDITIONAL
LOVE, GIVING ME THE
HOLY TRINITY, which makes me BETTER THAN BLESSED.

Oh What A Miracle!!!

BY: Evangelist Armetha Ingram

Oh, What a MIRACLE!
IN YOUR IMAGE, LORD, YOU made me.
LORD,, YOU gave me eyes to see.

Oh, What a MIRACLE!
LORD,YOU gave me a voice to talk.
LORD, YOU gave me legs to walk.

Oh, What a MIRACLE!
LORD, YOU saved my soul.
O' LORD, YOU made me whole.

Oh, What a MIRACLE!
O'LORD YOU gave me ETERNAL LIFE!
I THANK YOU, ALMIGHTY GOD, that YOUR GRACE SUFFICE.

I Can Do All Things Through Christ, Which Strengthened Me

BY: *Evangelist Armetha Ingram*

I can do all things through CHRIST, WHICH strebgthened me.
I don't listen to the devil, which tells me that I can't, don't you see?

For if he says that I can't, I show him that I can.
Then GOD takes me by my hand, and strengthens my inner man.

HE has given me HIS SPIRIT to preservere.
HIS PERFECT LOVE, (AGAPE LOVE) cast out fear.

So, in all boldness, I go forth in GOD'S WILL.
I serve one notice, that this boldness is not based on how I feel.

Forever God

BY: Evangelist Armetha Ingram

GOD is OMNIPOTENT, AND OMNIPRESENT,
ALL KNOWING, AND
EVERYWHERE.
SO, I serve you notice, that in all things, GOD is aware.
In all situations, HE is right there.
GOD will deliver you out of all afflictions, because HE cares.

GOD IS ALPHA AND OMEGA, THE
BEGINNING, AND THE END.
On ALMIGHTY GOD, one can depend
HE will deliver you out of your sin,
And will be with you unto the end.

At times, people can become strange,
But GOD never change.
GOD is the same today, yesterday, and forevermore,
FOREVER GOD, HE REMAINS THE SAME.
Yes, you can rely upon HIS HOLY NAME.

An Intimate Relationship With God

BY: Evangelist Armetha Ingram

What is an Intimate Relationship With GOD?
First of all, one must be totally sold out, and
surrendered to my GOD above.
The only way to accomplish this, is through THE AGAPE LOVE.

One must then possess the, "For GOD, I
Live, For GOD I Die," spirit.
Then one must Grucify Self, period.

All of this is accomplished through constant communication
with GOD through THE WRITTEN WORD, The Prophet,
PRAYER, and getting to know GOD'S voice, for one's self.
For GOD'S sheep will know HIS VOICE, and will follow none else.

God's Promises Are Guaranteed

BY: Evangelist Armetha Ingtam

GOD'S Promises are Guaranteed, for HE can not lie.
GOD'S COVENANT with HIS people, can not die.

HE is faithful to Perform that which HE has promised you.
If GOD said it, HE will see it through.

GOD'S WORD Is Settled In HEAVEN.
GOD Watches Over HIS WORD, And Is
Faithful Twenty Four Seven.

If You Believe It,
Then, You Shall Receive It.

If GOD Said It, Then Stand Upon It, And Savor.
GOD Will Not Alter HIS WORD; Plus HE Will Give You Favor.

In God's Secret Place

BY: Evangelist Armetha Ingram

He that dwells in The Secret Place Of The MOST HIGH, Shall Abide Under The Shadow Of The ALMIGHTY PSALM 91:1

In GOD'S Secret Place, we find shelter from the storm, and rain.
We find A REFUGE in HIM, in our affliction, and pain.

GOD Is Our High Tower; We Run Into HIS ARMS,
And HE Keeps Us From Harm, And All Alarm.

GOD Is Our ROCK OF OFFENCE.
HE Is Our Lawyer, Our Defense.

Yes, GOD Is Our Divine Protection; HE
Has A Fence, A Hedge Around Us
Every Day.
HE Continuously Keeps Us Out Of Harm's Way.

None But The Righteous

BY: Evangelist Armetha Ingram

*We are living in "THE LATTER DAYS," and
only the Righteous shall make it in.
It is time for you to get your house in order,
to be cleansed of your sins.*

*For JESUS is getting ready to CRACK THE SKY.
It is time to bid wordly pleasures, "GOODBY."*

*Will you be ready, when HE come?
Will HE find you with your work done?*

*Now is the Time For Salvation.
With GOD, You Need To Form A Relation.*

*The Earth Is Your Dressing Room.
So Get Prepared, To Meet The BRIDE GROOM. (JESUS)*

*Come to HIM With A Humble Heart, And A Contrite
Spirit, And HE Will In No Wise, Cast You Out.
Rest Assured Of This, Beyond A Shadow Of A Doubt.*

The Purpose Of, "More Than A Conqueror,"

TRIUMPH OVER TRAGEDY

The Overall purpose of my Book Of Poetry, Entitled, "MORE THAN A CONQUEROR," Subtitled, "TRIUMPH OVER TRAGEDY," Is For Inspiration, Encouragement, And To Save The Lost.

Made in the USA
Middletown, DE
05 May 2018